FIESTA!

TIBET

GROLIER

Reprinted 2006
First printed in 1999 by Grolier Educational
Sherman Turnpike, Danbury, Connecticut.
Copyright © 1999 Times Editions Pte Ltd. Singapore

Set ISBN: 0-7172-9324-6
Volume ISBN: 0-7172-9339-4

CIP information available from the Library of Congress or the publisher

7262

Brown Partworks Ltd.

Series Editor: Tessa Paul
Series Designer: Joyce Mason
Crafts devised and created by Susan Moxley
Music arrangements by Harry Boteler
Photographs by Bruce Mackie
Subeditor: Roz Fischel
Production: Alex Mackenzie
Stylists: Joyce Mason and Tessa Paul

For this volume:
Designer: Joan Curtis
Writer: Riga Wangyal
Consultant: Tibet Foundation, London
Editorial Assistants: Hannah Beardon and Paul Thompson

Printed by Everbest Printing Co. Ltd

Adult supervision advised for all crafts and recipes,
particularly those involving sharp instruments and heat.

CONTENTS

TIBET:

Tibet is now part of China and is called Xizang Zizhiqu by the Chinese government. It is a remote and isolated land, surrounded by the mountain ranges of the Himalayas, the Karakorum, and the Kunlun.

Ngari

First Impressions

- **Population** 2,280,000
- **Largest city** Lhasa with a population of 90,000
- **Longest river** Mekong
- **Highest mountain** Mt. Everest at 29,028 ft.
- **Exports** Gold, silver, copper, and zinc
- **Capital city** Lhasa
- **Political status** Autonomous region of China
- **Climate** Dry. Mild to cold weather.
- **Art and culture** A rich tradition of oral story telling. Important religious book called *The Book of the Dead*. Famous for dance and drama.

Nepal

Mt. Everest

India

▶**Many Tibetans lead nomadic**
lives, trekking the mountains with their animals as they search for food. They live in tents, easy to pack and carry when traveling. These tent-homes are covered in appliquéd stitchwork. Even city-dwellers have beautiful tents that they bring out for festive picnics and weekends in the country.

▶**This is the highest** country in the world, and the landscape is grand and mountainous. Many mountain climbers visit the country. These mountains lie just north of Lhasa, the capital city.

China

Tibet

Mekong River

LHASA

Samyai

Stiigatse

Bhutan

India

Bangladesh

▲**Yumbu Lakang castle** is the oldest known building in Tibet. Parts of it date back to the seventh century. Once the home of kings, it is now a Buddhist monastery. Buddhism is the religion of Tibet. The monasteries are not only temples in which to worship, but they are also centers of Buddhist teaching and history.

RELIGIONS

The Tibetan people are devout followers of Buddhism. They no longer fully control their own country, but they are determined to keep their traditional beliefs and culture.

BUDDHISM IS THE MAIN religion of Tibet. The other religion is Bon, which was the first religion of the people. Many Tibetan customs come from both sets of beliefs.

Buddhism was founded over 2,500 years ago in India, but was introduced to Tibet in the sixth century. Its followers worship Buddha, who teaches compassion and kindness to all living creatures.

Tibet is known to have over 6,000 monasteries and temples. Most Tibetan monks and nuns choose never to marry. Tibetan people are very religious. Most families have an altar where a statue or painting of Buddha and some religious texts can be found.

Usually, seven bowls of food, fruits, and water, and butter lamps are placed as offerings on these altars. Everywhere the people hoist their five-colored prayer flags on mountainsides, rooftops, shrines, and temples.

In 1950 the Chinese army marched into the capital city, Lhasa. There were small uprisings against the new masters. In 1959 the Dalai Lama, leader of Tibet, fled in fear from the country.

The Chinese destroyed many monasteries, and forced the monks and nuns to work on farms and factories. They wanted the Tibetans to forget their own religion and their old way of life. The Chinese even tried to make the Tibetans grow wheat instead of the traditional barley they always grew and ate.

The Chinese claim that Tibet is part of China. However, they have learned that the people of Tibet will not give up their own ways. Once more some temples are open, the faith has many followers, and monks are back in the monasteries.

GREETINGS FROM **TIBET!**

Tibet is known as the "Land of Snows." The country has many snowy mountains. The highest mountain in the world, Mount Everest, is in Tibet. For this reason Tibet is also called the "Roof of the World." It borders on India and Nepal in the south. Russia and Mongolia lie to its north, and China sits on the east. Most of Asia's biggest rivers, such as the Yangtse, Yellow River, Indus, and Brahmaputra, start in Tibet. It is almost twice the size of Texas. It has three provinces, U-Tsang, Kham, and Amdo.

There are many animals in Tibet. The yak is their national animal. Most Tibetans eat meat. Their diet is rich in dairy products. Barley is the staple food. It is roasted then ground into flour. This food is called *tsampa*.

They speak many dialects but with the same written language, Tibetan. A dialect is a variation of the main language. In the Tibetan language there are 30 consonants and four vowels. When Tibetans meet, they greet each other by bowing their head down, folding their two hands to the chest, and saying, "*Tashi dele*."

How do you say...

Hello

Tashi dele

How are you?

Keirang gusu

dipu yin bei?

My name is ...

Ngai...ming la

Goodbye

Galey pheb

Thank you

Thukje che

Peace

Shi dey

LOSAR

Losar *means "New Year." The calendar in Tibet is based on phases of the moon, and the people celebrate two "New Years."*

In Tibet *Gyalpo Losar*, which means the "King's New Year," is celebrated all over the country. It falls on the first day of the first month according to the lunar year. People just say "Losar" when they talk of this festival, but not when they refer to the second new year's day. This is the *Sonam Losar*, meaning the "Farmer's New Year." It falls on the first day of the eleventh month. It is, however, the King's New Year that is more widely celebrated.

Preparations for Losar begin at the end of the year. The women make new dresses. They clean their house and put up decorations. *Chang Kuel*, a barley beer, is now freshly brewed.

Before the festival begins, there are rituals

The weather is severe, and boots are designed to be warm and waterproof. However, they are also decorative. These men's boots are ornamented with braid.

Fur hats are essential in the cold winds of this mountainous land. During Losar people wear their prettiest hats for the festivities. Butter lamps and white scarves are laid on altars for the Buddha.

to bid farewell to the old year. These begin on *Gutor* 29. Gutor is the last month in the calendar of Tibet. Prayers are said, and a special broth is prepared.

Remains of the broth are mixed with dust and a little dirt from the house. This mixture is then placed where two roads or paths cross. This ritual act is to chase away any bad or negative aspects of the old year so the new year starts hopefully.

Losar is a time when the girls and women wear their prettiest clothes. Good food is prepared and is eaten with the *Chang.* The party begins in the early morning when people greet each other with the words *Tashi dele.* This means "good luck and prosperity." They offer *chemar,* a mix of tsampa, sugar, and butter.

In the temples the faithful make offerings to the Buddha. These are placed on elaborate altars. Afterward they

Ornament in Tibet is rich with color, and the natural world inspires many designs. These women's boots are embroidered with fanciful flower emblems.

THE POWER OF PRINT

Prayer sheets are carefully wrapped in beautiful cloth. In Tibet printed words and drawings of holy subjects are treated with great respect. The lines on the page carry a deep power. Passages from holy writing are printed onto flags. These are hoisted on hills, on roads, and in fields. It is believed the words will rise to the heavens where they will be received kindly. Those who put up the flags, or pass them with reverence, will be blessed. This custom of placing offerings and praying outdoors probably started long before Buddhism. In those ancient times offerings were made to natural forces such as the wind, the rain, and the sun.

The close tie between humans and the natural world is clear in Tibetan art. A candleholder in the temple is modeled from an animal's head.

give alms to the poor they meet in the streets.

This is a time when people renew their faith. They pray to Buddha to bring them good fortune, and they promise him that in the new year they will be kind to others.

Religious dancing and music are performed in courtyards of the large temples and monasteries. Monks can be heard chanting, and the air is filled with the sounds of bells and gongs. New, colorful

This painted container is filled with rice and barley. Corn ears are thrust into the grains. The whole arrangement is a symbolic hope for a prosperous new year.

During Losar the Buddha may receive simple gifts or rich offerings such as this ornate butter lamp.

prayer flags are hoisted on rooftops.

In the courtyards of wealthy homes folk operas and storytelling sessions take place. The streets are filled with people in beautiful, new clothes. Entertainers and musicians can be seen everywhere.

On the second day of Losar Tibetans visit their family and friends. They exchange gifts. The day passes very pleasantly, with stories about the Buddha and songs. Families gamble and play traditional dice games.

There are song contests and performances of folk music for entertainment. Celebrations for Losar are planned to start the year in a happy, hopeful way.

Double-sided drums are popular. They are struck with a curved stick. Cymbals are very much part of temple music, where their loud sound frightens bad spirits or announces grand ideas of birth and death. All kinds of music are heard during Losar.

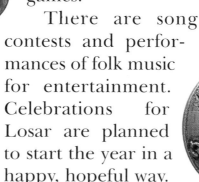

MAKE TIBETAN BEADS

The Tibetans are famous for the colorful and heavy jewelry the women wear.

Tibetan women wear beads hanging on their necks and arms. They ornament their hair and decorate their belts with loops of beads and discs. The beads are of amber and other semiprecious stones. Heavy silver discs are frequently mixed with the beads. Our necklace and belt ornaments are made of painted clay.

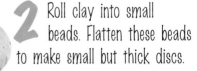

YOU WILL NEED
Air-hardening clay
Poster paint
All-purpose glue
7 20" lengths of wool
Toothpicks
Brushes for paint and glue

1 Roll air-hardening clay into small beads. The shape and size of the beads need not be regular, but keep them similar. Pierce the center of each bead with a toothpick. Allow to dry. Paint the beads. When dry, varnish with all-purpose glue.

2 Roll clay into small beads. Flatten these beads to make small but thick discs.

3 Pierce center of discs with toothpick. Allow to dry. Paint discs. Varnish with glue. Knot one end of length of wool. Thread alternating beads and discs. Tie both ends of wool. Cut and neaten ends.

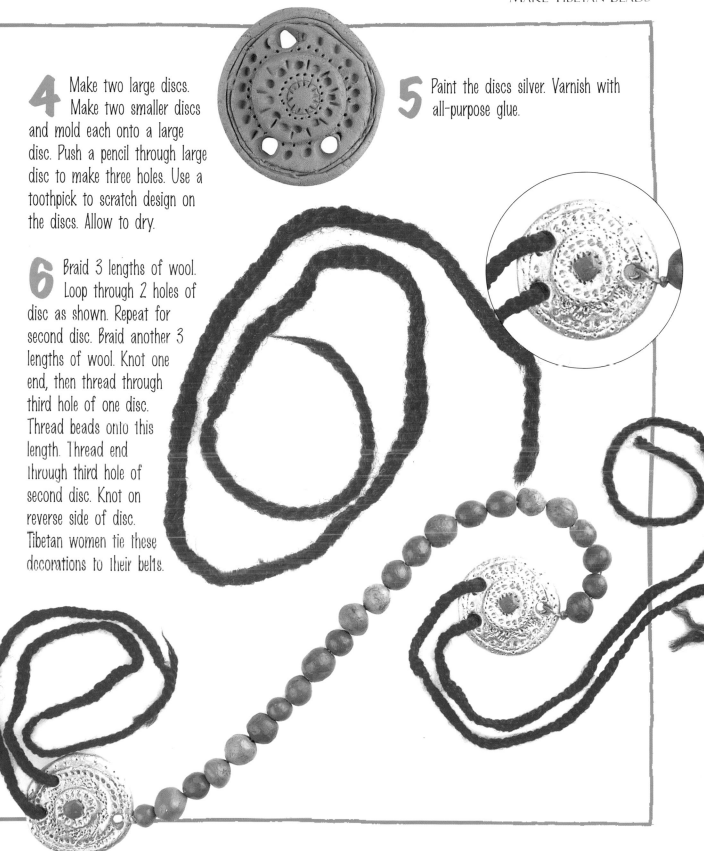

4 Make two large discs. Make two smaller discs and mold each onto a large disc. Push a pencil through large disc to make three holes. Use a toothpick to scratch design on the discs. Allow to dry.

5 Paint the discs silver. Varnish with all-purpose glue.

6 Braid 3 lengths of wool. Loop through 2 holes of disc as shown. Repeat for second disc. Braid another 3 lengths of wool. Knot one end, then thread through third hole of one disc. Thread beads onto this length. Thread end through third hole of second disc. Knot on reverse side of disc. Tibetan women tie these decorations to their belts.

SAGA DAWA

This is a festival to celebrate the life, the learning, and the serene spirit of Buddha. It is a serious day but also one of joy.

Noble women wear heavy, ornate jewelry in the Saga Dawa procession.

Buddha Day, called *Saga Dawa,* is the most important day of the year. It falls on the fifteenth day of the fourth month of the lunar calendar.

The Buddhists of Tibet believe that this day marks the birth and the enlightenment of Buddha. It also celebrates *Parinivana.* This means the death of Buddha, when he went into a permanent state of peace.

Saga Dawa is a time that inspires young and old to study their faith and think about the great Four Noble Truths of Buddha. The faithful think about his lessons on the spiritual world.

The Buddha in the "Earth-touching posture" that symbolizes the roots of wisdom and the defeat of ignorance.

PRAYER WHEEL

Prayer wheels help the faithful communicate with the Buddha. The prayer wheel is a hollow cylinder. Inside it are sheets of printed prayers, or *sutras,* as the Buddhists call them. Each time the wheel is rotated, it has the same power as actually saying all the prayers. Most prayer wheels are hand-held or hand-turned and are placed in fixed rows around temples. However, some may be turned by water or heat. They are treasured objects and usually adorned with patterns and symbols.

Many hundreds of Buddhists prostrate themselves at their temples. This means that, as they pray, they lie face downward on the ground. They chant prayers to Buddha. After visiting the temple, people make generous offerings to the poor. It is said any good deeds done on this day are a thousand times more virtuous than those done on other days.

In the capital city of Lhasa government offices are closed for the day. Officials on horseback form a procession through the streets. They visit the main temple and the winter palace, Potala, that belongs to the Dalai Lama.

Bells can be heard at all times in Tibetan temples. Craftsmen make sure the bells are carefully made and richly decorated.

Then they make their way to his summer palace, Norbu Lingkha. Tibetans love their horses, and the animals in the parade are decorated with bells, tassels, and colorful scarves. Even their saddles are beautifully decorated.

The grand parade ends at a lake called Dzongyab Lukhang. This lake is believed to be home to water goddesses, the givers of rain and water.

This lovely lake is a favorite boating and picnic area.

15

TIGER POWER

Tigers are associated with nobility in Tibet, and the animal is believed to be the spiritual guardian of the Tibetan elite. The shape and colors of the animal are often used in decorations or woven into the design of carpets. The symbolic power of the tiger is so strong that the pattern of its fur is enough to evoke its presence.

On Saga Dawa people line the banks to watch the richly decorated boats of officials and noble families sail across the waters.

Religious music and folk songs entertain the watching crowds. The instruments include mouth organs, flutes, lutes, and oboes. Displays of folk dancing from the different regions of Tibet are performed on the lakeside.

Children play the game of *thepe*. Players use a shuttlecock made of a piece of lead or slate wrapped in a cloth with feathers attached to it. They keep the shuttlecock in the air by kicking it with the sides of their feet. The one who keeps the shuttlecock in the air for the longest period is winner.

Saga Dawa is the time when all the people display their faith. The nobles show their respect to Buddha

This amulet is of the kind worn by men. An amulet is attached to clothing. The image of the Dalai Lama reminds believers of their spiritual leader on Earth. He is the man who guides them on the true path of Buddha.

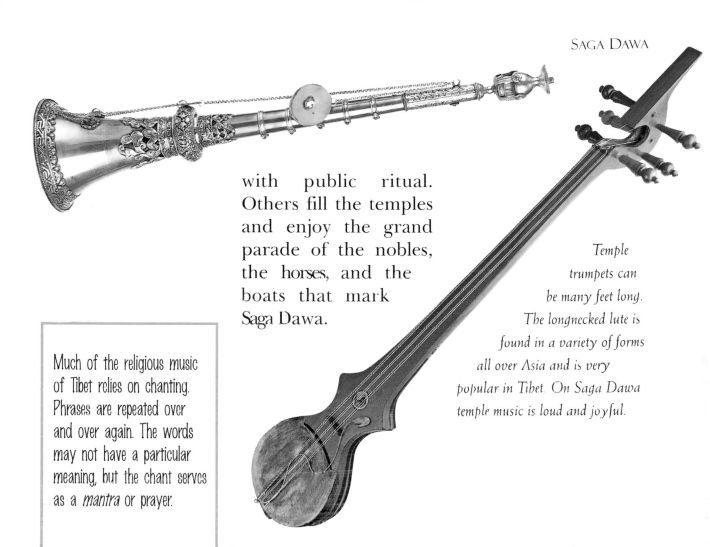

with public ritual. Others fill the temples and enjoy the grand parade of the nobles, the horses, and the boats that mark Saga Dawa.

Temple trumpets can be many feet long. The longnecked lute is found in a variety of forms all over Asia and is very popular in Tibet. On Saga Dawa temple music is loud and joyful.

Much of the religious music of Tibet relies on chanting. Phrases are repeated over and over again. The words may not have a particular meaning, but the chant serves as a *mantra* or prayer.

OM MANI PADME HUNG

Pad - me Hung Om Ma - ni Pad-me Hung Om Ma-ni Pad -me Hung Om Ma -ni

Pad - me Hung Om Ma - ni Pad - me Hung Om Ma -ni Pad -me Hung

ALL LIFE IS SACRED

Buddhism teaches that all life is to be honored and that we should not kill. This folk tale promises rich rewards to those who follow Buddha's lessons.

ONCE IN A SMALL village in eastern Tibet there was a family who had three daughters and one son. They were very poor, and the father made a living as a hunter. The father wanted his son to learn how to hunt, but the son refused to kill. The family worried that they would all starve when the father was too old to hunt.

One day the father took his son hunting. They saw a big hare near a rocky cave. The father was very pleased. He took his sling out to kill the hare, but his son started to shout and chased the hare away.

The father was very angry. He took a big rock in his hand and began to shout at the child. "You are my only son, but you are absolutely no good to the family. I will kill you."

The boy ran off. He hid in the nearby cave that was too narrow for his father to enter. The cave was dark, and the boy was frightened. As his eyes grew used to the dimness, he saw a distant opening. He crept along until he came to the opening.

The boy saw a lovely meadow and some monks sitting on a riverbank. The senior monk told him they were on a pilgrimage to holy places, but the boy was welcome to join them.

During their travels they met the boy's youngest sister. She was so pleased

to see her lost brother she gave him a magic horse that could talk. The boy thanked his sister and went on his way with the horse.

The boy was very alarmed when the horse whispered in his ear to say, "You must kill me and spread my skin on the ground. Place my heart, lungs, and liver at the four corners of the compass, and scatter my hair in the air so the wind blows it in every direction."

The boy refused to kill the horse, so during the night the horse threw itself over the cliff.

The next day the boy cried when his horse did not come to greet him. When he found the dead horse, he was very sad. He remembered what his horse had told him, so he followed the strange instructions. The boy prayed for the horse before he went to bed. The next day the boy found that the horse's skin had been turned into a grand castle. Its innards had become chests of precious jewels. Each hair had changed into an animal.

The monks told the boy that this was his reward for refusing to kill another living being. They sent the boy off to seek his old parents. When he reached home, his mother was very pleased to see her lost son safe and well. The father wept and asked for forgiveness.

The son hugged his father and told him, "All life is sacred."

He took the old couple to live in his castle. From that time on the father stopped hunting and dedicated his life to Buddha. The loving family all lived in peace and harmony.

ZAMLING CHISANG

This festival mixes elements of the old beliefs of Bon and the ceremonies of Buddhism. It is a day of picnics and horse rides.

Zamling Chisang is Purification Day, celebrated on the fifteenth of the fifth lunar calendar. This is believed to be when Samye, the first monastery in Tibet, was built in A.D. 800.

This festival contains elements from the old religion of Tibet. The old beliefs are called *shamanistic*. This means a belief in gods, demons, and the spirits of the dead. People were able to contact these various beings only through a *shaman*, which means a priest or priestess.

This old religion is called Bon. In ancient times the believers of Bon always roamed the hills during this season. They felt some hills and mountains had magical properties. The trips were made on horseback.

The ritual of the journey became part of the Buddhist calendar and is now included in

Sticks of incense with a silver incense holder are part of the equipment carried into the magical hills during the Zamling Chisang festival. Dragons are considered signs of good luck. Their image may be found all over Tibet.

YOGURT AND RICE DESSERT

Cook the rice according to the manufacturer's instructions. While the rice is hot, add the raisins.
Add the butter cut up in small pieces and mix well with a wooden spoon. Put the rice into a bowl and add the sugar and yogurt. Stir well, but be careful not to mash the rice.
Serve in dessert bowls.
This dish can be eaten hot or cold.

SERVES FOUR

1 cup uncooked white rice
½ cup raisins, brown and white
3 oz. butter
2 T. sugar
1 pint plain yogurt

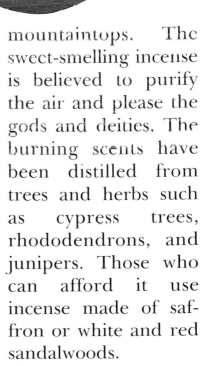

Zamling Chisang. Tibetan Buddhists still make this journey to the mountains and hills of their country. They travel on horseback, and the occasion has become a great excuse to show off people's skills in horse riding. Parents often choose this occasion to give children their first solo ride on the back of a horse.

While treking through the hills, the faithful place burning incense sticks in incense burners all over the slopes and on mountaintops. The sweet-smelling incense is believed to purify the air and please the gods and deities. The burning scents have been distilled from trees and herbs such as cypress trees, rhododendrons, and junipers. Those who can afford it use incense made of saffron or white and red sandalwoods.

Prayer flags are hoisted from tents and

PRAYER FLAGS

Prayer flags are made of thin cloth. Each flag is of one color only, but five colors are used. These are: red for fire, green for water, yellow for Earth, blue for the sky, and white to symbolize clouds. On each flag Buddhist texts are printed around a central motif of a horse. At each corner there is an animal. There will be a lion in one corner, a tiger in another, then a dragon, and a *garuda*, a kind of mythical bird. Tibetans believe the wind carries the blessings of the texts to the heavens and across the world.

Lion figures, sometimes distorted to make them look fierce, have a symbolic value. They are given powerful qualities. For instance, they are believed to stop evil spirits of the dead harming the living.

shrines. They flutter across hillsides and are planted on remote moutaintops.

Temple rituals are part of this day. The music of Tibet is composed to have certain effects. There is music to call or banish good and bad energy. Other chantings and sounds are meant to take the spirit away from the body and allow it to travel through the heavens.

This music is often very loud and harsh, although the deep chanting of the monks can be tranquil.

When the ritual journey and temple services are over, everyone takes the opportunity to enjoy the holiday. Many have picnics that can last for four to five days. Lhasa is filled with pilgrims. Families from across the land

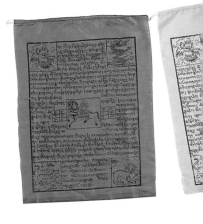

often tells a mythical story or an old legend. Sometimes the words may be modern and make clever political comment.

This music is a strong element of life in Tibet, and singing may be heard all the time. However, when it is a festive day like Zamling Chisang, the people relax and sing even more than usual.

The Wind Horse sits in the middle of the prayer flag. It carries the jewels of Buddhism on its back, and it is a symbol of good luck. Tibetans love their horses and for Zamling Chisang decorate the animals as lavishly as this Wind Horse.

gather and camp in beautiful Tibetan tents pitched in the public parks.

Street operas and folk musicians can be seen and heard everywhere. When men and women are together, the singing alternates between each group. They sing rhythmical refrains to each other. The folk music of Tibet

THE YAK KEEPER'S DAUGHTER

*The girl's beautiful voice as she sang the old songs
of Tibet enchanted her animals. It also brought her
love and happiness.*

ONCE UPON A TIME there was a family who had only one daughter and many herds of yaks and sheep. Her name was Gawa, and she was very pretty and always kind and obedient to her parents. She was good and helpful to her neighbors and everyone liked her. She looked after the herds, and she used to take them to high places where the grasses are rich and fresh.

The animals liked her too. She used to talk to them and was clever when any one of them was ill. She enjoyed looking after the herds, and she used to chant the old songs so beautifully the animals waited eagerly every day for her. Even a Yeti, one of the solitary, strange creatures who live up mountains, far from others, waited daily for her melody. He fell in love with her.

Now, one day Gawa was not very well. A boy was to take the herds that day. However, when he called the animals, they would not follow him. The elders tried as well, but the animals refused to move.

The next day Gawa was a little better and insisted she would take the herds. Her parents were worried that she might fall ill again, but they let her go. In the afternoon Gawa got very ill. She was all alone with her animals. They were upset but did not know how to help her.

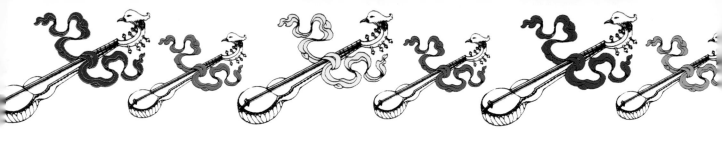

The oldest yak decided to seek help from the Yeti up the mountain, while the other animals gathered around Gawa to keep her warm. The old yak found the Yeti and told him the whole story.

The Yeti gathered some herbs and came to help the sick girl. He attended to Gawa very lovingly and gently, and soon she recovered. All the animals were really happy because they all loved her.

Gawa thanked the Yeti for his kindness, but the Yeti asked her if she would marry him! Gawa said she had to look after her parents and animals, but the Yeti promised to look after them.

When the girl returned home, she told her parents that she wished to marry the Yeti. They were shocked and sad that their only daughter wished to marry a Yeti. The old folk loved the girl. They wanted her to be happy so they gave her their blessing.

The very next day Gawa went to the Yeti to tell him she wished to marry him.

All the animals were very happy. Although the Yeti was tall and big and hairy, he was kind and as gentle as a lamb. The animals gave milk and wool to Gawa's parents so they were happy. The girl and the Yeti were married and lived happily ever after.

WANGKOR

This festival is the farmers' special day. It is hard growing crops and keeping animals in the cold mountains and valleys of Tibet. This is the time to thank the gods for the harvest.

In the countryside *Wangkor* is of great importance and is celebrated by every farmer. It occurs when the crops have ripened and been harvested. It is a religious festival, a time when the deities are thanked by the farmers. It is also a welcome holiday from farm work.

The date of Wangkor varies from region to region but usually it falls within the first two weeks of the seventh month of the Tibetan calendar. The farmers prepare for the festival by printing new prayer flags and making new clothes. Quantities of food are organized for the day.

On the chosen day each community of farmers puts up tents in the fields and hoists its new prayer flags around the campsite. Entire families, all in new clothes, gather together in the field and pray to Buddha. They also send prayers to the lesser gods and other deities.

The stronger men in the company then lift onto their backs a load of Buddhist texts, along with a statue of Buddha and one or two other holy figures. Then they must walk right around the field. This task must be done before the sun is set. The statues are placed on a campsite altar.

Incense of juniper leaves is burned before the altar. Everyone holds some *sangphud* in their right hand. This is a mixture of barley flour, butter, and honey. The whole company chants a prayer then throws the mixture into the air. After this ritual the party starts.

Food and drinks are served. People sing and dance in the field.

Yaks are important farm animals. They are used to carry burdens and as transport for people. Their milk is drunk and made into butter. A pretty saddle blanket on this yak celebrates Wangkor.

The next day is filled with archery contests and horseraces. The children wrestle and run races. Winners and losers get prizes, so the Wangkor party is a happy one.

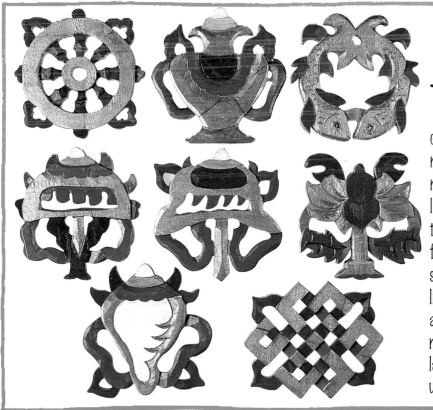

SACRED EMBLEMS

The Eight Sacred Emblems of Buddhism are painted everywhere, even on the walls of remote farmhouses. In the top row is the wheel, the cycle of life, then the vase of hidden treasure. The fish symbolize the free swimming of the soul. The second row has a banner for life, an umbrella for protection, and a lotus for growth. The last row has a conch shell for language and a knot for the unity of the spirit.

MAKE A TIBETAN MASK

This mask is a copy of a Tibetan mask, but any colorful design can be painted on the shape.

YOU WILL NEED
Large square corrugated cardboard
Masking tape
White wall paint
Poster paint
All-purpose glue
Sheets of newspaper
¹/₄ yard fluffy fabric

Tibetan Buddhists display cloth paintings of the Buddha in their temples and on family shrines. These paintings are called *thangkas*. Sometimes a huge thangka may be hung outdoors. People wearing masks perform ritual dances before the Buddha image. The masks symbolize various deities and spirits and they make the wearer feel "invisible."

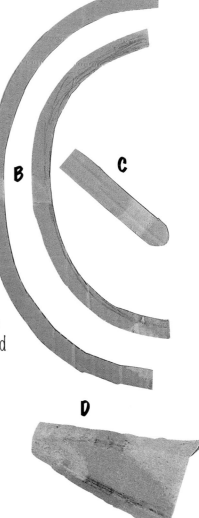

1 Draw the shape of your mask on corrugated cardboard. Make it big enough to cover your face. Cut out the shape.

2 Cut cardboard into semicircles about ¹/₂" width, one (A) long enough to fit outer rim of mask and one (B) to fit inner curve.

3 Cut out strip (C) about ¹/₂" wide. Cut triangular nose shape (D).

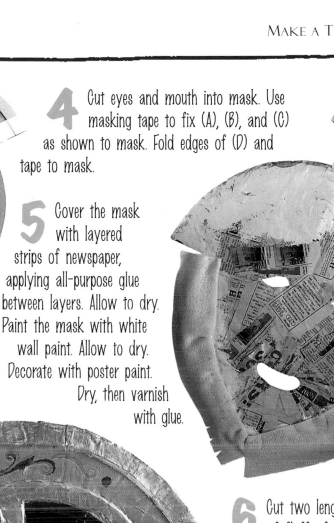

4 Cut eyes and mouth into mask. Use masking tape to fix (A), (B), and (C) as shown to mask. Fold edges of (D) and tape to mask.

5 Cover the mask with layered strips of newspaper, applying all-purpose glue between layers. Allow to dry. Paint the mask with white wall paint. Allow to dry. Decorate with poster paint. Dry, then varnish with glue.

6 Cut two lengths, 2" wide, of fluffy fabric to fit length from crown to chin of mask. Trim fluff off $1/7$" strip along one edge of each length of fabric. Snip along trimmed edges. Glue snipped edge to reverse of mask, easing fabric around curve of mask.

7 Attach elastic thread with tape to reverse side so that it fits onto head.

THANGKA FESTIVAL

Monks wear masks to dance before huge images of Buddha displayed at the monasteries of Tashilhunpo and Dreprung.

Tashilhunpo Monastery is near Shigatse city in central Tibet. For only three days of the year the monks display three huge *thangkas*, cloth images, of Buddha. These are displayed on the temple's vast Thangka Wall, nine storys high.

Tibetan Buddhists celebrate the vision of the thangka and believe it has holy qualities. Monks perform *Cham*, ritual masked dances before the thangkas. Pilgrims, with offerings of *tsampa,* or barley meal, come to witness the images. A similar ceremony occurs at the Dreprung Monastery in south Tibet.

WORDS TO KNOW

Alms: Gifts of food or money to the poor.

Altar: A table on which worshippers leave offerings, burn incense, or perform ceremonies.

Buddhism: A religion based on the teachings of Gautama Buddha, who lived in India in the 5th century B.C.

Chanting: A way of praying. Buddhists memorize long prayers and chant the words out loud, often in groups.

Dalai Lama: The spiritual head of Tibetan Buddhism.

Deity: A god or goddess.

Dialect: A regional variety of a language.

Emblem: An image, shape, or sign that symbolizes a belief or idea.

Enlightenment: In Buddhism, the attainment of a state of supreme spiritual wisdom known as *nirvana*.

Incense: A mixture of gum and spice, often shaped into thin sticks or cones, that gives off a pleasant smell when burned.

Lunar calendar: In this calendar a month is the time between two new moons — about 29 days.

Monastery: A place where monks live in a religious community.

Monk: A man who devotes his life to his religion and lives in a monastery.

Pilgrim: A person who makes a religious journey, or pilgrimage, to a holy place.

Prayer flags: Flags with holy writing on them. These flags are hoisted in the belief that the words will rise to the heavens.

Prostrate: Lying face downward.

Shamanistic: Followers of shamanistic religions believe in a hidden world of spirits who can be contacted by a priest or priestess known as a shaman.

Shrine: A place sacred to the memory of a holy person.

Temple: A place of worship. Buddhists worship in temples.

ACKNOWLEDGMENTS

WITH THANKS TO:
The Tibet Foundation, London.

PHOTOGRAPHY:
All photographs by Bruce Mackie except: John Elliott p. 21.
Cover photograph by Robert Harding Picture Library.

ILLUSTRATIONS BY:
Alison Fleming pp. 4 – 5. Robert Shadbolt p. 7. Maps by John Woolford.

Recipes: Ellen Dupont.

SET CONTENTS